SURVIVAL

'How fear works'…
Journal

LOUISE L. KALLAWAY

SURVIVAL
How fear works

First published in Australia by Louise L. Kallaway 2024
louiselkallaway.com

*A catalogue record for this
book is available from the
National Library of Australia*

ISBN: 978-0-6459194-2-4 (pbk)
ISBN: 978-0-6459194-3-1 (ebk)

Typesetting and design by Publicious Book Publishing
Published in collaboration with Publicious Book Publishing
www.publicious.com.au

Front cover image: Pictrider © (shutterstock)

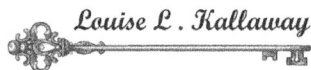

Louise L . Kallaway

I dedicate *Survival* to your primitive personal bodyguard and to everyone with the courage to embrace their fear and transcend survival intel from a 21st C. intellectual perspective.

Other Life Education books:

- Empowered – Secrets of Your Inner Child

- Defiance – Secrets of Your Midlife Crisis

- Evolving – Secrets of a child and life processes

- You and Your Inner Child Today – Journal

- Conscious – 'How life works' – Journal

Fear is a primal survival force. Fear was programmed into your primitive DNA and forms part of your *reactive* survival intelligence. Its primal focused job is dedicated to your physical safety. This program remains unchanged today.

THE POWER MENU:

THE GIST

Since life began, fear has been part of our survival DNA. Fear has been drummed into us as little kids, drummed into us by Society and the status quo, marketing with its 'missing out' fears, the dramatic, fearful daily news, climate change etc.

We take over our *fear of fear* as maturing adults with such fears as:

- fear of judgement/fear of criticism/fear of rejection

- fear of embarrassment/fear of humiliation/fear of ridicule

- fear of failure/fear of success

and on it goes.

Until now, fear has generally been viewed as an opposing force and fundamentally anti-expansive. Let's liberate ourselves and the 21st Century with new, empowering insights into our primal fear and its reactive survival bodyguard intelligence.

INTRODUCTION

Hello and welcome. Thank you for your trust, courage and support.

Fear! Even the word conjures up powerful anti-expansive reactions, doesn't it? But what if I said, 'without knowledge of the survival system we were born into, we have been relating to fear the wrong way!'

My books and journals are based on 30-years of research into the non-intellectual survival system we inherited. The aim of my 'life education' books and journals is to *bridge the gap* between primitive survival intelligence when there was no intellect and the 21st C., simplifying, deepening and empowering our understanding of life from a 'whole of life' perspective.

'The survival System' was designed for a life expectancy between 20 – 35 years. Today the maturing adult is living two, three, even four times longer than our primitive cousins, stunted and held back by 'The system' time forgot!

I am not a psychologist. I am a researcher and this is my Calling. I have found no evidence to suggest psychology plays a role in any survival programs.

My 30-year research collated the basic programs in the survival system that are evident in our lives today. The *reactive* survival programs were essentially to get out of harm's way fast helping us survive a hostile environment and a much shorter lifespan. Without the aid of an intellectual brain which evolved much later, the survival system had to be reactive/kneejerk... no thinking required!

There have been no changes to the primitive programmed survival system.

They still operate as:

- survival reactions e.g., 'fight or flight' responses to fear.

- when your subconscious identifies a similar situation from the past that is happening in current time, *you react.* In an instant, you know what to do, what you believe, how you feel, your attitude etc.

Caveman… fast, kneejerk, repetitive, reactive behaviours… no thinking required!

These behaviours are basically copied behaviours learnt in childhood from the previous generation/s. *Generational cycles repeating themselves.*

When you consider our lives are based on 85% – 90% subconscious reactions, I think you'll agree, it would be in our best interests to know how the system works.

From an intellectual perspective, a better understanding of fear and its key role in our survival will help to soften the way we feel towards fear, acknowledging its powerful and predictable presence *and our subconscious 'second-hand reactions' remembered from an earlier time zone.*

***

I have added a couple of lined pages at the end of each Section for your notes/challenges.

I like to use the masculine 'he' or 'him' rather than he/she or him/her. There is no gender bias. It simply makes for an easier read.

I speak to you in *italics*, regularly checking in on how you are feeling with this empowering information.

An important distinction: the child I am referring to throughout this journal is a child born some 30, 40, 50 or more years ago, not today's child.

Should I touch on anything that causes you concern, please consult with a trusted friend or counsellor. **I point out that your confidant may be part of the status quo and go into denial.** Watch for any signs of resistance.

Now let's build a new and empowered understanding of *your* relationship with your fear.

PART 1

THE PROGRAMMED SURVIVAL SYSTEM OF LIFE

SECTION I:

SETTING THE SCENE

1. FEAR AND YOUR PROGRAMMED SURVIVAL

From the hunters and gatherers of primitive times to the hi-tech, intellectual world of the 21st Century, our lives are governed by the exact same ingenious, non-intellectual survival intelligence!

In its most simple, basic form, what is survival?

- Survival is eat, sleep, drink... procreate. Repeat.

- Behaviours copied from the previous generation/s.

- No thinking required! On-autopilot!

A few simple examples of our primitive programmed life:

- Our primal Will to survive translates into an innate 'Need to belong' to help us survive. **'The system' we were born into empowered 'The Pack'.**

- Fear of abandonment is a primal fear and **remains unchanged today.**

- Fear and its 'fight or flight' *reactions* were borne into our DNA. **No change to this *reactive* survival program.**

- The subconscious mind was our *reactive and repetitive* primitive memory, before our intellectual brain began evolving. **Today, the subconscious is still our memory in the first seven years of our lives, before our intellect takes over!**

- We were born self-protective with our feelings, senses and instincts operating, making us aware of our current situation. Fear warned us of impending physical danger. **No change to this program.**

You can see from the above shortlist how 'hardwired' survival programs are still directing our lives today and that's just the tip of the iceberg.

What has changed?

- We now live two, three, even four times longer than our primitive cousins.

- Our intellectual brain continues its development until we are around 25 years old and is now only 10% - 15% evolved. *Having trouble accepting this one?*

- Today, with our much longer lifespan, 'The individual' is emerging… especially in midlife, but he is being held back/intimidated by our unconscious and innate 'need to belong' and its all-powerful 'Pack' mentality/conformity expectations aka today's status quo.

The 'survival system' cannot be switched off! Until now, most of us have been living in reactive survival mode and 'on autopilot'.

To power-up and make sense of your life, let's find out more about 'The system' and the two time zones running simultaneously.

2. THE TWO TIME ZONES OPERATING IN YOUR LIFE

To deepen and broaden your understanding, let's acknowledge the two time zones referred to in Aristotle's famous quotation:

"Give me a child until he is seven and I will show you the man."

Aristotle was an Ancient Greek philosopher C 384 B.C. – 322 B.C.

This quotation has been around for 2300 years! and holds a massive key to our understanding and to the evolution of life.

I have frustratingly discovered: most adults don't believe, flatly refuse or full-on deny that their childhood has any connection to their adult lives! I watch their eyes glaze over at the very mention of the 'inner child'.

How do you feel about the term 'inner child'?

....

....

....

Denial that we live in a survival-based 'two-time zone system' and that we have an inner child, is holding up our evolution. To counter this denial, I have respectfully renamed the 'inner child', your subconscious 'backseat driver'. We all know what 'a pain' a backseat driver can be, don't we?

How is it possible to be living in two time zones?

- The first seven years establishes our unique 'childhood model' i.e., our blueprint for life. *Have you heard of the childhood model? No? I hadn't either. The next chapter will explain.*

- The literal beliefs of the childhood model and copied generational behaviours learnt in the first seven-years of our lives are hardwired into our *reactive, repetitive* subconscious mind/memory.

- When your subconscious recognises a belief or a situation that is similar to what is happening in present time… without prompting or thinking, you instantly 'know' what to do, what you believe, how you feel, your attitude etc. No thinking required!

'The survival system' at work: instant, subliminal, unconscious, subconscious repetitive *kneejerk reactions* – the two time zones and one reaction!

Your evolving intellectual brain is not part of your hardwired survival beliefs put together in the first seven years. We are living our programmed lives on *reactive, repetitive* subconscious survival memory. In other words, we are living on autopilot, programmed for survival! This system is only concerned with your survival and continues ad *infinitum…* whether you embrace its existence or not. *'The system' is winning so far!*

The first seven years of our lives establishes our survival beliefs i.e., the foundational beliefs for the whole of our lives until we read one of Kallaway's books or journals! No joke!

For more understanding, let's investigate our childhood model of life.

3. THE CHILDHOOD MODEL – YOUR BLUEPRINT FOR LIFE

The literal childhood model of life is formed in the first seven years, *before our intellectual brain* takes over. The childhood model contains hardwired subconscious survival beliefs and copied behaviours that essentially form the foundations for the whole of our lives.

Did you know you have a childhood model of life? That your children in the first seven years are establishing their childhood model? And your grandchildren will also assemble their childhood model… all unique to each child.

Debriefing the contents is one of the most empowering and liberating experiences of our maturing lives. What can we expect to find in our childhood model of life?

- Generational themes, values and attitudes.

- A 'Need to belong' to survive.

- Everything we observed, heard and felt repeatedly.

- Copied generational behaviours.

- Learnt coping behaviours e.g., staying of the spotlight

- A need to fit in and conform.

- Fear and its comfort zone boundaries.

- Little, if any, reference to time and change.

- Standards, controls and limitations.

- Should, should not, must and supposed to beliefs.

- No self-responsibility.

- No alternative choices – we lived in a yes-or-no, right-or-wrong, either/or world.

- Feelings of powerlessness/helplessness.

- No sign of independence.

- A serious, personal world with no humour about ourselves.

- Resentments.

- Images and beliefs about us that were formed from the opinions and feedback from others.

As a literal little kid, we believed everything at trusting face-value. Even though there is no factual data to back up our literal childhood beliefs, those hardwired beliefs live deep within our subconscious mind, trapping us in a tiny 'personal' serious world, with fear establishing our comfort zones. Those beliefs, unless intercepted, potentially become our forever subconscious backseat driver and our adult self-fulfilling prophesies. *Okay with this?*

When you were young, you didn't know or understand that:
- Fear
- Your 'Need to belong' and
- Emotional dependence on 'The group'
had the power to usurp your individual and maturing development.

Living in childhood model constraints will always leave the adult with feelings of self-doubt, not enough, compromised and powerless.

From the childhood model concepts listed above, which subjects are most likely holding you back today?

....

....

....

How are your should, should not, must and supposed to beliefs impacting your life? Any you can update? Release?

....

....

....

Can you think of any benefits you gain by living in your childhood model?

....

....

....

Viewing your childhood as a temporary learning experience, rather than remaining unconscious, unacknowledged and permanent, introduces a powerful new adult perspective and huge possibilities for your future potential.

Now let's find out how and why we repeat generational cycles.

4. REPEATING GENERATIONAL CYCLES

Like mother, like daughter; like father, like son. Children are copycats! What did you see, hear and feel repeatedly? We usually don't remember but our subconscious never forgets!

Why your childhood becomes your children's childhood:

In the adult time zone, without awareness, we unconsciously and automatically repeat behaviours we saw frequently in our childhood. Everything a child observes, hears and feels repeatedly, is their version of 'normal'. "*This is how life works and this is what I do*" is how the little kid in you deems life should be... forever. *The two-time zones.*

Without intellectual involvement, your hardwired reactive subconscious mind will repeat your literal childhood beliefs and observed copied behaviours, e.g., Domestic violence, unconsciously repeating generational cycles, *ad infinitum.*

The child eventually becomes the adult and then possibly a parent who will repeat his learnt, copied childhood behavioural patterns subconsciously, automatically and unconsciously to his children. And so, the generational cycles – good, bad and indifferent, continue repeating themselves. *It's confronting, isn't it? How are you feeling?*

Let's find out more about your pro-life subconscious mind, how it works and how it relates to the whole of our lives from a survival perspective.

5. AN UNDERSTANDING OF THE SUBCONSCIOUS MIND AND SURVIVAL

Although there are many books available on how to work with the subconscious mind, I now wish to add more understanding and its importance in our lives from a *survival, repetitive, reactive perspective* and how it relates to our lives today.

Did you know?

- The subconscious mind is pro-life and has been helping us survive since the beginning of time.

- The subconscious mind was our primitive survival memory.

- **The subconscious is still the survival memory in the first seven years of every child's life, before our intellectual brain is sufficiently developed to take over!**

- **The subconscious mind does not recognise or respond to the intellect *ever*... no matter our age, stage or status in life!**

- The subconscious has a harmonious and unified relationship with emotional intensity.

- The subconscious mind lives in its own time zone i.e., it does not live by man's manufactured time. There are no clocks or watches in its world.

- The subconscious does not conform to man's rules.

- Your subconscious is always on alert... dedicated to you.

Your subconscious mind has been compared to a literal six-year-old child:

- It cannot reason, question, discriminate or make distinctions.

- It lives in its literal world, believing everything you say, trusting you and your words, especially those spoken with emotional intensity – *be careful what you say and be careful what you wish for.*

- It loves repetition and images.

When you think of your subconscious mind, think of a literal, serious, 'personal' six-year-old child living in its own time zone.

How to work with your subconscious mind today is covered in Section VI: Your courageous emotional bases.

A distinction between a subconscious reaction and a memory:

Subconscious reactions are fast, automatic and subliminal, reacting to previously formed beliefs and behaviours that are similar to your present situation, directing you to act in some way.

Memories are *reminders* of something from your past – good, bad or indifferent. They are usually attached to your senses e.g., the smell of a roast dinner cooking taking you back to childhood family gatherings, a song reminding you of someone, a joyful event, a sad occasion etc.

6. IDENTIFYING YOUR NEED FOR SECURITY

To help you progress, it's important to have an up to date understanding of your need to feel secure. I might add here, feeling safe is one of our most cherished feelings, not only in childhood but throughout our lives. No wonder our bodyguard had (past tense) such an easy time!

We are all born self-protective and security-conscious, helping us survive. Add fear and we have a potent cocktail and very sound reasons why it's been so difficult to break away from our programmed security-conscious behaviours.

How and what do you need to feel safe and secure?

....
....
....

If you feel a 'Need to belong' to a particular group, or any groups, is this need coming from a sense of love, obligation or loyalty to the group? Or is it driven by fear i.e., their reaction if you show signs of independence? *Please give these questions deep thought as they contain a lot of your key answers:*

....
....
....
....
....
....
....
....
....
....
....
....

The following list of questions are designed to find out your current need for security and to help shift your awareness. There are no right or wrong answers:

Do you choose to stay in your comfort zones? Reasons:

....
....
....

Do you complain about things not working out for you? Are you willing to try something new?

....
....
....

Do you fear self-expression? Any examples? Reasons:

....
....
....

Do you question your authority figures or your peer group? Or do you remain silent? Reasons:

....
....
....

Have you questioned the beliefs and values you were brought up to believe? Are they relevant today?

....
....
....

Do you fear change? Reasons:

....

....

....

Do you constantly seek the company of others? How do you feel about spending time alone? Reasons:

....

....

....

Do you make concessions, justifying or excusing other people's behaviours? Reasons:

....

....

....

Do you stay 'as sweet as pie' hanging onto your anger and resentments? Or do you voice how you are feeling (softly and gently). Reasons:

....

....

....

Can you hear any powerlessness in your answers?

- Are any answers linked to your backseat driver's 'Need to belong'?

- Not wanting to rock the boat?

- Avoidance or blaming?

- Accepting there's nothing you can do about the situation... just accept it.

For a very long-time avoidance was my way of dealing with life, but it left me feeling powerless, that I'd missed a great opportunity to own up… especially to myself.

Today… you are not powerless but coming from your backseat driver's literal security-conscious childhood model of life, you feel powerless.

You are so much more than your inner child could have imagined – your backseat driver is still living in its childhood time zone and its fear-based comfort zones. Your inner child is the one 'stuck' in its childhood… not you!

In the next Section, we'll disarm 'live' subconscious reactions to show you the massive differences between the time zones. All good news!

Notes/challenges:

....
....
....
....
....
....
....
....
....
....
....
....
....
....
....
....
....
....
....
....
....
....
....
....
....
....
....
....
....
....
....
....
....

PART 2

YOUR CHILDHOOD/ADULT
TIME ZONE

SECTION II:

DISARMING 'LIVE' SUBCONSCIOUS REACTIONS/ RESPONSES

OVERVIEW: THE TWO TIME ZONES

This Section will make you truly aware of your immense parenting power in the first seven years of every child's life.

Automatic subconscious reactions behave like contractual cords unconsciously tying us to the primitive survival system forever or until we become conscious.

We can never cut/severe the cords to our hardwired subconscious survival beliefs, the beliefs formed in the first seven years, but we can disarm their 'live' power with new awareness. This is how our adult intellect can build a 'dream-team' Higher consciousness with our inner child/backseat driver.

Prepare yourself for a massive shift in your awareness. There can be no going back to childhood powerlessness after reading this Section! Let's begin with our innate 'Need to belong'.

7. THE 'NEED TO BELONG' – AN INNATE FORCE

Belonging to the 'Pack' kept us safe and protected and was the caveman's way of surviving.

Today, our innate 'Need to belong' and dependence on 'The group' in the first half of our lives, becomes an unconscious intimidating force as we mature.

Let's find out how this new understanding fits in with our lives today:

Childhood years:

In a nutshell, our very survival depends on someone caring for us, doesn't it? Our primal Will to survive translates into a 'Need to belong', to be loved and cared for. *Abandonment is a primal fear.*

Teenage years:

Teens shift alliances from the tribal family to their generation. *Exclusion, rejection or non-acceptance from their peer group, feeling like they don't fit in or belong with either group, is dangerous territory for teens.* That's how important a sense of belonging and its emotional support is, in the first half of our lives.

The unaware/reactive adult:

The unaware/reactive adult feels confused and 'stuck'. He wants a bigger life, but he doesn't understand 'The system'. Fear, his need to belong and dependence on others for emotional support intimidates this individual and holds him back from acting independently. Feelings of 'stuckness' is one of the first signs that his emotional life is ready to expand and support him.

Empowered concepts:

This maturing adult acknowledges his yearning for independence. He understands the two time zones and realises he no longer 'needs to belong' for childhood survival or for his teenage generation's support and acceptance. Emotional dependence on others interferes with his maturing position and belongs to the past. Acknowledgement of his liberated and empowered position; that he is now a separate and complete entity, allows him to make emotionally independent choices to progress his life, the adult rite of passage... if he has the courage.

Do you feel pressure to conform? Where is this pressure coming from? How is it impacting you?

....
....
....

Affirmation:

*"I am a separate and independent adult with a Will of my own.
I honour my maturing needs."*

8. YOUR 'NEED TO BELONG' AND THE STATUS QUO TODAY

Let's find out how our childhood and teenage 'Need to belong' for survival and acceptance respectively, keeps the unaware maturing adult toeing the line with his generation and the wider status quo and 'their' conformity expectations.

The unaware/reactive adult:

The unconscious adult has little understanding of his innate need to belong. Fear of rejection, fear of self-expression and criticism or judgement from 'the group' and its 'Pack' mentality/conformity keep him in his fear-based comfort zones, emotionally stunted, not living up to his potential for *fear* of upsetting family, friends, neighbours and relationships' wider social circles.

Empowered concepts:

Today, the aware adult rationalises that he no longer needs to belong for survival or acceptance. It is his duty of care to himself and his rite of passage to make independent choices that transcend his need to belong and its conformity issues to fulfill his maturing needs; *seeking his own approval, not just above peer group approval, but above status quo approval per se! Huge!*

What are you *not* doing for fear of upsetting others?
....
....
....

What would you like to change? Tiny steps.

....

....

....

It's as simple as it is complicated, isn't it?

Affirmation:

> **"Working with my fear and self-approval,**
> **I honour my maturing needs."**

9. EMOTIONAL DEPENDENCE

We never really think about the issues arising from our emotional dependence on important others, do we? It's another big one:

The literal child and emotional dependence:

The need to belong and emotional dependence on the tribal family for survival is a basic requirement for every child. Knowing that our carers love us and emotionally support us, the child feels protected and understood, affirming that he is okay. *Love this!*

The unaware/reactive adult:

The unaware/reactive adult has not reconciled that his need to belong, emotional dependence on his tribal family and a need for his generation's acceptance keeps him fitting in and conforming, adding to his feelings of frustration and powerlessness. He finds it difficult to stand up, to say what he wants or needs, and he doesn't understand where his feelings of 'stuckness' are coming from.

Empowered concepts:

This adult understands the two time zones and now intercepts childhood beliefs that are not working for him today. He adjusts his coping behaviours to fit his maturing stage of life, becoming aware of his patterns, and reviews and updates his self-image. ***He is no longer reliant on others for emotional support and to feel okay about himself.*** He can lean on himself and endorse his own approval! *Huge!*

Will this new understanding change your life? How?

. . . .

. . . .

. . . .

Affirmation:

*"Emotional independence from group
conformity liberates my freedom."*

10. CONFORMITY

We have a love/hate relationship with conformity, don't we? It's a double-edged sword. We feel safe living in the fold, but it's also stunting our potential. Let's dig deeper:

The literal child and conformity:

The literal, powerless, dependent, security conscious child has no understanding of conformity. You, me and all the other little kids were programmed to conform. Primitive behaviours such as 'follow the leader', the concept of safety in numbers and fitting in were part of our upbringing, basically to maintain 'order' and to help us survive. Fair enough, but this doesn't allow a child to feel like an individual. *Is this where we got the idea that we didn't fit in anywhere?*

The unaware/reactive adult:

This adult doesn't understand that fear, his childhood survival beliefs, dependence on peer group acceptance and its 'Pack' mentality/conformity, are all contributing to his feelings of 'stuckness', frustration and powerlessness. He even squashes his maturing needs and his potential, for fear of upsetting family, friends and wider social circles, adding to the chip on his shoulder. *Conformity sucks the power from this individual.*

Empowered concepts:

This maturing adult is aware of primitive tribal, generational and societal conformity conditioning. He also acknowledges and respects his emotional maturing needs. *He reasons that he is not rebelling against his generation or the status quo, but rather, choosing to make independent decisions that work in his best interests today.* **He is transcending his fear of fear of**

rejection, while acknowledging deeper survival and acceptance issues that will open his world exponentially – the awakened adult's rite of passage.

What beliefs do you have about conformity? Are you intimidated by the thought of your peer group's reaction if you choose a different path to their expectations?

....
....
....

How big could your life be without conformity issues? With a little bit of courage, what's the first thing you could change to own your power?

....
....
....

Affirmation:

> *"Conformity sucks the power from my life.*
> *I transcend my childhood and teenage need to conform."*

11. FEAR

Until we understand and accept the concept of the two time zones operating in our lives, we will continue to automatically *react* to fear via our inner child's 'second-hand' subconscious reactions to fear, plus add-ons since then!

Let's see how the above understanding plays out in our lives today.

The literal child and fear:

The literal, security conscious little kid in us wants to feel safe and knows instinctively to obey fear. Every time fear was present, we usually retreated. Fear set our comfort zone boundaries. Our inner child's intellectual brain was not sufficiently developed to make a distinction between a real fear and/or a perceived 'what if' fear.

The unaware/reactive adult:

This adult is unaware of the two time zones active in his life today and doesn't understand where his fear is coming from. He continues to be managed and limited by fear and its intimidatory survival tactics. His emotional life remains on hold as he continues to live frustratingly in his comfort zones and under his potential. Anxiousness and 'settling' will most likely become a way of life for this individual.

Now it's time to strap your backseat driver into the front passenger seat next to you and begin to intellectually *respond* to fear.

The empowered adult:

The empowered adult has become aware that his fear uses all types of intimidating strategies and tactics to keep him safe. He acknowledges his feelings of fear and questions the type of fear he is experiencing; he usually discovers it is a perceived 'what if' childhood fear rather than a physical, real, present-day fear. He assures his fearful backseat driver: ***'I've got this; I'll keep you safe'* to reduce the little kid's anxiousness and the adult's 'second-hand' reaction to fear.** *Love this!*

The empowered adult also acknowledges with his new intellectual insights that every time he chooses to expand his comfort zones or when he moves towards or into unknown territory, he will automatically feel anxious and fearful. He can now progress with his bodyguard accompanying him, as it should... no longer the Master of his life.

What are your tell-tale signs fear is present? Where do you physically feel fear? e.g., your solar plexus?

....
....
....

Every reaction to fear is pre-empted by a thought. What were you thinking immediately before fear presented itself?

....
....
....

What circumstances push your fear buttons?

....
....
....

Did you know, fear loves surprises? It's in its element when you are surprised by an unexpected outcome. *It really is a menace, isn't it?*

Affirmation:

> *"I acknowledge fear to reduce its intensity.*
> *I use 'self-talk' to build my confidence.*
> *I do not retreat!"*

How to handle your fearful emotional reactions will be covered in Chapter 16 and we'll address self-talk in Section IV.

Reassurance:

How are you feeling? A little confronted or overwhelmed? Trust me: I did too! I was in my late fifties when I came to the Gargantuan realisation that I had lived most of my life as Aristotle's classic seven-year-old child!

Although I had the advantage of discovering my inner child and its model of life gradually, I still refused to believe and accept that I was feeling and behaving as a child, which held up my work for two more years! as I tried valiantly to disprove my research and analytical concepts, even though the evidence was abundantly clear and made perfect sense of my life.

If you are interested in learning more 'You and your inner child today' Journal reviews 31 subjects, including those above, written in a slightly different format. I believe this a first; an opportunity for your 'backseat driver' to speak to you giving its literal version on each of the subjects in its childhood model.

I now invite you to connect with the dynamics of *your* fear in Section III.

Notes/challenges:

....
....
....
....
....
....
....
....
....
....
....
....
....
....
....
....
....
....
....
....
....
....
....
....
....
....
....
....
....
....
....
....
....

....
....
....
....
....
....
....
....
....
....
....
....
....
....
....
....
....
....
....
....
....
....
....
....
....
....
....
....
....
....
....

PART 3

YOUR PRIMAL FEAR AT WORK TODAY

SECTION III:

THE DYNAMICS OF FEAR

OVERVIEW: YOUR PERSONAL BODYGUARD AND SURVIVAL INTEL

Welcome to more insights into your primitive personal bodyguard.

We now know: fear's job is to keep you *physically* safe. It does this by sending you silent warnings e.g., feelings of uneasiness, anxiousness, butterflies, 'fight or flight' adrenaline responses. Your repetitive/kneejerk subconscious, also dedicated to your survival, *reacts* to your current situation by repeating similar past experiences. You could easily view this as another example of the 'two against one system', couldn't you?... helping you survive.

In this Section, we'll begin with a brief understanding of the two sides of your brain, acknowledging the intellectual areas missing from your childhood model, and we'll cement the reasons why fear is a second-hand reaction and how/why adrenal fatigue is on the move today.

How to cope with your fearful emotional reactions, making sense of how fear and avoidance band together to keep you safe and how to manage your fear and self-doubts are all covered in this Section.

12. THE BRAIN

To add more clarity to the intellectual parts missing from your childhood model, let's briefly check the differences between your right-side feeling brain and your left-side intellectual brain.

'She' the right-side emotional/feeling brain has been part of our primitive survival intelligence since life began – before the intellectual brain began evolving.

The right-side brain:

- is the female or yin side of our brain.

- controls the left side of your body.

- she is the emotional, 'personal' feeling side of your brain.

- she is intuitive; she does not think.

- she is 'all-knowing' with access to Higher consciousness.

- she is creative, imaginative and able to visualise.

- she is non-competitive.

- she bases herself on expansion and abundance.

- has a harmonious relationship with the subconscious mind.

The left-side brain:

- is the male or yang side.

- controls the right side of our body.

- he is 'impersonal'.

- he is the logical, reasoning side of the brain.

- he is competitive.

- contains the ego, that likes to think of itself as an individual, separate from others.

- he sources his knowledge from outside himself.

- he identifies the image he has of himself through others.

- he bases himself on scarcity and limits.

- he is analytical and problem-solving.

The intellectual left-side of your brain is a relative newcomer. He was not part of our primitive survival intelligence, and he is still not part of our survival intelligence today! The literal beliefs from the first seven years of every child's life are hardwired into the subconscious memory – no intellect involved.

Using both sides of your brain today – emotional intelligence and intellectual intelligence is the balance of Yin/yang – the Chinese 'complete'.

13. WHY FEAR IS A SECOND-HAND REACTION – AN INTELLECTUAL PERSPECTIVE

Without an intellectual understanding, fear remains life's greatest oppressor.

Fear and its primitive survival agenda continue to protect you. Nothing has changed. Fear is on your side although, I admit, it does have strange ways of showing it. ☺

No matter our age, stage or status in life,
we are a work in progress.

Expansion means your personal bodyguard
will always be present –that's its job!

Know this: The fear you felt as a child, which kept you safe and in-line, is the same fear you are feeling today. Until we understand the concept of the two time zones operating in our lives, we continue automatically reacting to fear via our backseat driver's 'second-hand' subconscious fearful reactions.

In other words, the fear you are feeling today is not your adult fear – it is a subconscious second-hand reaction to fear that is repeating perceived 'what if' fears from your childhood that are still trying to keep you safe. **Remember: as a child, you had no intellectual brain to respond to fear, only a child's *reaction* to fear. You will be reminded of those fears every time you make choices to expand your life.**

I discovered that my resistance to change or trying anything new was usually based on perceived fears from childhood i.e., the 'what if' variety rather than real fears. My fears then translated into my avoidance behaviours. 'Ah-ha!'

Now let's find out how your body interprets your everyday stressors as fear and the subject of adrenal fatigue.

14. WHAT'S ADRENAL FATIGUE/BURNOUT GOT TO DO WITH FEAR?

After years of living with diagnosed 'low-grade anxiety', then a high dose of radiotherapy in 2010, my adrenals and I were completely burned out! Two long years later, without much improvement, I booked into a local homeopath. Her remedy had me up and on my feet with renewed energy in a few short months!

As mentioned on the back cover, fear is primal, simple and basic and therefore has limits. You are not dealing with an intellect: you are dealing with an entity that doesn't understand nuances.

We usually don't associate modern-day stress with fear. Let's find out how fear interprets/misinterprets modern-day stress as a physical danger impacting your precious reserves of adrenaline. Primitive body/21st C. stress.

At time of writing, adrenal fatigue or 'modern day burnout' is slowly becoming a recognised medical syndrome. Your two tiny adrenal glands are located on top of each of your kidneys. They supply your body with adrenaline, among other things. It is part of your para-sympathetic nervous system. *When you are chronically stressed (tired and wired), adrenaline sympathetically reacts, helping you cope with your stress levels.* Those reserves of adrenaline, once used to prepare your body for physical danger, are being set off by everyday stressors.

In other words, primitive 'fight or flight' reactions to fear are being activated by modern-day lifestyles. Primal fear and your primitive body cannot tell the difference between physical danger and chronic modern-day stress.

The fundamental problem is: When you feel stressed for long periods of time, your para-sympathetic nervous system is not given enough rest and recovery time between high adrenaline demands to build its precious reserves, resulting in an imbalance between the two nervous systems.

When you are suffering from adrenal fatigue, a complete change in attitude and lifestyle is often the only long-term answer. Type A personalities are particularly prone to adrenal burnout.

Reviewing how you deal with the stressors in your everyday life will help you live within your primitive, physical confines and remain healthy, strong and energetic.

Let's find out what's causing your high adrenaline demands, and what you can do to reduce your stress levels. Should you wish to investigate adrenal fatigue further, there are some excellent books on this subject.

Highlight any of the following physical symptoms of fear that may be a daily constant in your life, without any *real physical danger*:

feeling under pressure/stress	constantly pushing yourself
feeling uneasy, anxious, tense	tightness in your chest
hyperventilating	sleep problems
constriction/lump in your throat	neck and shoulder tightness
intensity e.g., high excitement	panic attacks
over-stimulation	palpitations

Any others?

....

....

....

Where in your physical body do you feel stress? e.g., solar plexus, stomach?

....

....

....

Let's go deeper and understand the tactics your fear uses to help you survive.

15. YOUR FEAR AND ITS COVERT MULTIPLE PERSONALITIES/IDENTITIES

As mentioned in the last chapter, I was diagnosed with 'low grade anxiety'. I eventually discovered that many of my anxieties were perceived 'what if' fears coming through my subconscious mind every time I encountered similar situations in present time from my past experiences. The two time zones.

Without an intellectual response to the way you react to stress/fear, it becomes your way of dealing with life. Because your fear often disguises itself as something else, it's best to understand its tactics.

Does your fear appear as:

- aggression

- confusion

- feelings of intimidation.

Any others?

....
....
....

Does your fear use delaying tactics such as:

- procrastination

- indecision

- avoidance

- self-doubt.

Any others?

....
....
....

Here are some more ways fear may appear in your life *without any real physical threat:*

- fear of ridicule

- fear of being on your own

- fear of humiliation or embarrassment

- fear of consequences

- fear of not speaking up, not saying what you want or need

- fear of rejection

- fear of questioning an authority figure or your peer group

- fear of success

- fear of owning up to your part in a scenario

- fear of failure

- fear of the unknown.

Any others?

....
....
....

What are the tell-tale signs your stress/fear is present?

....

....

....

Is your stress related to physical danger or your current stressful situation? e.g., are you expanding your comfort zones?

....

....

....

What situations intimidate you, cause you to feel overwhelmed or nervous?

....

....

....

Do you lose interest or avoid if you feel intimidated? Is this a pattern?

....

....

....

As revealed in Chapter 11, every feeling is pre-empted by a thought! What were you thinking *immediately before* you became aware of *your* fear?

....

....

....

What causes stress or anxiety in your life? e.g., technology, public speaking?

....
....
....

What can you do to overcome your stressors/anxieties mentioned above?

....
....
....

Is there anything you avoid so you feel less stressed? e.g., speaking up?

....
....
....

Is aggression part of your fear response? What presses your buttons?

....
....
....

Does indecision or procrastination result in anxiety for you? Do you then make a quick decision to eliminate this feeling? Is this a pattern?

....
....
....

Is there anything you fear facing? Reasons:

....
....
....

Here's a seemingly disparate one. When you are feeling highly excited by what you are doing or anticipating, does your fear interpret your excitement as tension/stress activating your adrenals... feeling like you are on a high?

....

....

....

I discovered that when 'we' are expecting a certain outcome, but suddenly we get something different, fear appears! As mentioned earlier, surprise is fear's ally.

Use the above questioning whenever you suspect your fear is hindering your progress. Your adrenals will thank you too.

To give you a little more to work with... when I'm feeling overwhelmed or anxious:

I write down everything that is causing my stress. I can then see what my 'monkey mind' and my over-active intellectual mind are worrying about. They have usually bundled everything together without any filters e.g., they haven't determined priority or urgency, they haven't separated the things I'm working on from the miscellaneous items I could diarise to do soon etc. I can then thank my busy mind and assure myself that there's nothing to worry about! It's a great and simple way of alleviating stress levels. Please try it.

16. HOW TO COPE WITH YOUR FEARFUL EMOTIONAL REACTIONS:

Now... you are in charge! You can decide whether to react subconsciously (the way of a child) or respond intellectually (the way of an adult). This is another massive difference between the two time zones.

Remember: for survival reasons, your childhood is about safety, security and certainty. When the adult pushes through his childhood comfort zones, he will feel his inner child's fearful reactions. It's practically guaranteed!

What can you do to assure yourself and pacify your anxious backseat driver? Try saying this to your inner child:

"I feel your anxiousness. I've got this! You don't have to feel frightened anymore. I'll keep you safe; we're a team now! Let's move forward and find out what life has to offer. I promise, I'll take care of you."

Today, you are taking charge of 'unexpected', overwhelm, panic, stress and all fearful *reactions* relating to your current situation. A shift in awareness connects you to your adult *'responding'* power base and this time zone.

Try doing this with your intense feelings:

When you become aware of an intense feeling – you don't need to know in this moment what triggered the feeling, simply identify and acknowledge the feeling: *'I feel ....'*. Watch it lose its power and strength as you resonate with the feeling. *Quite amazing.* **It's like standing up to a bully!**

Depending on the intensity, you may have to acknowledge the feeling several times… but it works! I believe, that acknowledging your feelings, especially your intense feelings, is one of the best kept secrets of life. More power to us!

Try acknowledging fear, anger, rage, frustration or any other severe emotional reactions! As those feelings lose their effect/impact/strength and intensity, you become the one in charge!

As I said earlier: Most of us want to feel safe and secure, not just in childhood but throughout our lives, which is another reason why fear is so intimidating to most of us. *Adrenaline junkies may disagree!* ☺

Worth repeating:

> *"I acknowledge my fear to reduce its intensity."*

17. HOW FEAR AND AVOIDANCE BAND TOGETHER TO KEEP YOU SAFE

Avoidance comes under the umbrella of self-protective behaviour. It is another coping strategy. When we can't cope or when we feel powerless or simply not up to it, we avoid. I call it 'avoidance hibernation'. Avoidance is so common today, there is a personality type known as the 'avoidant personality'.

Avoidance seemed easier to me, but there was always a nagging feeling that I'd let myself down. In retrospect, there were many things I didn't understand about avoidance and its consequences, especially how my avoidant behaviour and fear were 'ganging-up' and blocking any sense of my personal power.

Do you fit the 'avoidant personality' profile? Let's check some examples of fear and avoidance:

- avoiding issues you know will cause you pain and/or discomfort

- postponing change or making important decisions

- being afraid to ask questions of a VIP or your authority figures

- avoiding changing jobs or careers, even though you are miserable

- avoiding speaking up

- not asking for assistance

- not acting on your intuition

- not standing your ground
- not taking risks – even well-considered risks
- avoiding situations that threaten a relationship you value
- not making doctor, dentist appointments etc.
- staying in relationships or careers that no longer satisfy you.

Any others?

....
....
....

What does avoidance or withdrawal from life *feel* like and *sound* like?

- "Everything is too big for me to handle at the moment."
- *"Everything is too difficult."*
- "I'm not up to it; I can't do this right now."
- *"I can't cope with all the pressures I'm feeling."*
- "If I withdraw, hopefully, they won't ask me again."
- *"If I stand up and no one agrees with me, I will feel humiliated."*
- "I don't want any more responsibility."
- *"I just want to do what I need to do to get by."*
- "I don't want to rock the boat. I want people to like me."

- *"I want to keep the peace."*

- "I don't want to draw attention to myself."

- *"It's easier to keep quiet and be the nice guy."*

- "It's better for everyone if I don't create more problems."

- *"I don't want to risk losing important relationships if I voice my opinion."*

- "I don't want to be on my own."

- *"It's safer not to know. What can I do about it anyway?"*

Any others?

....
....
....

How do you feel when you avoid what's happening in your life?

....
....
....

People don't know what's important to you when you don't let them know – always softly and gently.

Can you see how closely aligned avoidance is with the different types of fears mentioned in Chapter 15? *Interesting, isn't it?*

18. HOW TO MANAGE FEAR AND SELF-DOUBTS

*"Fear is not an opposing force; fear is a
primal, self-protective survival force."*

Louise L. Kallaway.

Here's a list of techniques to help you manage your fear and self-doubts:

- Remind yourself fear is primal, simple and basic and therefore has limits. You are dealing with an entity that doesn't understand nuances; it is dedicated to your physical safety.

- Imagine fear as your personal bodyguard always on alert, watching out for you and know it is on your side.

- Assure and pacify your frightened inner child. Let him know you are taking charge and dealing with fear, creating a bigger future together.

- Work with your fear and its multiple personalities/identities and the strategies and tricks it uses to keep you safe, as listed in Chapter 15.

- Breathe. Deep abdominal breathing helps to keep your mind calm and your body strong.

- Get in touch with your neck and shoulders. Need to shrug a few times to loosen them up?

- Acknowledging your fear will help to reduce its severity. You may need to repeat this acknowledgement several times until you ultimately take control.

- Become aware of your internal dialogue. We'll cover self-talk and affirmations in the next Section.

- **Remind yourself that a fearful reaction is expected when you are expanding your comfort zones or moving into unknown territory.**

- Write a list of everything that is causing your stress to help put your worries into perspective.

- Try a few simple yoga poses. Thinking the 'Corpse pose' and the 'Child's pose'.

Any others?

....

....

....

Notes/challenges:

....
....
....
....
....
....
....
....
....
....
....
....
....
....
....
....
....
....
....
....
....
....
....
....
....
....
....
....
....
....

SECTION VI:

COACHING SUCCESS

OVERVIEW: THE VOICE OF PERSONAL POWER

Motivating and coaching yourself to success is the voice of your personal power.

Positive self-talk is a great fear diffuser and can be likened to the way a paramedic speaks softly and gently to someone needing comfort and emotional support.

Positive self-talk and affirmations are powerful portable allies, available 24/7, helping overcome self-doubt, childhood insecurities and emotional obstacles, whenever you need encouragement and motivation.

Your inner child with its Will to survive craves security and certainty and has manufactured with its instincts, senses and feelings, a haven. Fear reminds you every time you are pushing its boundaries... if you leave its comfort zones, how will you survive?

In other words, you have two fearful reminders trying to stop you from advancing... your inner child and fear! The two against one system... again!

Failure

We learnt about failure in childhood, that failure was somehow shameful.

Perhaps we remember failure as an embarrassment – the little kid in you being laughed at and embarrassed in front of everyone. Fear and your subconscious continue to remind you of those types of incidences, and we know your backseat driver craves security and certainty, don't we? Trying has no certainty! Again, 'The system' is keeping us emotionally stunted and inhibited.

Today, trying is success! without the need for certainty.

Let's find out how positive self-talk and affirmations can open a new world of possibilities for you.

19. SELF-TALK AND AFFIRMATIONS

You know your personal bodyguard will always be in the background doing its job, and you know your childhood subconscious survival beliefs will continue to present their kneejerk reactions to your current situation. Let's counter these reactions by adding the kind of motivational phrases that will encourage you to take the next step.

Highlight the phrases below that resonate with you:

- 'I love taking charge of my life.'

- *'My fears are perceived fears. They can't hurt me.'*

- 'The next step will be so empowering.'

- *'I love conquering my fears.'*

- 'My fears and self-doubts are mostly from childhood.'

- *'I'm ready to take on more responsibility.'*

- 'I am transcending my childhood self-doubts.'

- *'There is no such thing as certainty. Trying is success.'*

- 'I understand how fear works and what is holding me back.'

- *'I adapt to change easily.'*

- 'I am ready and willing to go beyond my childhood limits.' *(Love this!)*

- *'I am bigger than this situation. 'We' can do this!'*

- 'I am a winner and loving it!'

- *'I am so much more than I ever dared to believe.'*

- 'I can handle anything that comes my way.'

- *'I am ready to face my future with new confidence.'*

Any others?

....

....

....

Continue to encourage yourself. Talk softly, gently and lovingly to your inner child: *"Come on kiddo, we can do this! We're a great team."* You are becoming your own life coach and creating your future today.

Congratulate yourself regularly on your continuing progress.

20. RANDOM QUOTES ON FEAR:

To assure you that fear effects all of us, the following quotations are a reminder that fear is universal:

"Fear defeats more people than any other one thing in the world."
Ralph Waldo Emerson.

"Fear are stories we tell ourselves."
Unknown.

"Feel the fear and do it anyway."
Jack Canfield.

"Everything you want is on the other side of fear."
Jack Canfield.

"You gain strength, courage, and confidence by every experience in which you really stop to look at fear in the face... do the thing you think you cannot do."
Eleanor Roosevelt.

"All our dreams can come true if we have the courage to pursue them."
Walt Disney.

The following is an excerpt from a most-loved quotation by Marianne Williamson from her 1992 self-help book 'A Return to Love':

"Our deepest fear is not that we are inadequate.
Our deepest fear is that we are powerful beyond measure.
It is our light, not our darkness that most frightens us.
We ask ourselves, Who am I to be brilliant,
gorgeous, talented, fabulous?
Actually, who are you not to be? You are a child of God..."

Do you have any favourite fear-based quotations? Please add them here:

....
....
....
....
....
....
....
....
....
....
....
....
....
....
....
....
....
....
....
....
....

Now let's find out how fear and the status quo 'gang-up' on you.

Notes/challenges:

....
....
....
....
....
....
....
....
....
....
....
....
....
....
....
....
....
....
....
....
....
....
....
....
....
....
....
....
....
....
....
....
....

SECTION V:

HOW FEAR AND THE STATUS QUO 'GANG UP' ON YOU

OVERVIEW: YOU, FEAR AND 'PACK' CONFORMITY

First, the philosophy of 'The Pack' aka today's status quo will always be *'one rule fits all'*, *'united we stand, divided we fall'*:

- it must *always* be their way

- they don't like to be questioned or challenged

- they don't like change

- they are completely set in their ways

- they don't like people rocking their boat!

- keeping everyone average and mediocre is a major principle.

In other words, it's all about control. The controlling nature of the status quo goes back to the primitive survival system; our need to belong to the 'Pack' and its 'Pack mentality'… keeping us safe. But now, our intellectual brain can question, challenge and decide whether conforming with the crowd is still in our best interests, or if there are more beneficial, empowering ways for the individual to live independently today.

Know in advance that if you stand up and say what you want or need or challenge any of their rules, as far as they are concerned, you are causing them problems. They won't change! Everything was fine before you spoke up. See how it works? One on one or a group situation, it's always the same. The defensive ones make it personal and begin to attack you. Their intractable mindset means they will never look at their role in any scenario or be willing to negotiate a more conciliatory outcome with you. The words 'negotiation' and 'conciliation' are not in their vocab.

We need to review and challenge the way we've been conditioned to think. The so-called non-conformists are evolving – moving forward, leaving the rest of us behind!

21. THE STATUS QUO – WHO ARE THEY?

Let's find out in a humorous way who the status quo may be:

- are they old fogeys who sit in judgement, gavel in hand, and insist that everyone lives their lives in the past using old perspectives?

- are they younger, still clinging to their security blankets and living in their childhood comfort zones?

- is their world 'personal' and serious like a child?

- have they not heard of negotiation and conciliation?

Do you have any questions for them? Remember, they don't like questions:

....
....
....

The status quo and fear will always see themselves as your protector. This is another 'two against one' system helping us survive... before we could think!

Fear, in its many forms, dictates the philosophies of the status quo. Do any of the following statements sound familiar?

- 'This is the way we do it. This is the way it's always been done and the way it will be done in the future.'

- 'We rule – it's always been that way. We know how it works so you can feel secure.'

- 'This is the safe version of how you should live your life.'

- 'Don't give it another thought – we have the situation under control.'

- 'You don't have to worry about changes – there will be few, if any, on our watch.'

- 'You must never cross the line – we may not be able to rescue you. Better the devil you know.'

- 'You'll love the stability of our leadership.'

- 'You must be loyal to your tribal family, your generation and all their rules – they are always working in your best interests.'

- 'Remember – every rule is for your benefit.'

- 'When you break the rules, you risk jeopardising your position among us.'

- 'We are the last word.'

Does it sound like a parent speaking to a child or a young adult? Can you think of any other statements you've heard?

....
....
....

All humour aside now, what does the status quo offer the individual?

- The status quo gives the member a sense of security.
  Your inner child craves security.

- The status quo creates the image of solidarity and certainty. **Your inner child craves certainty.**

- The status quo can almost promise the individual that there will no change/s. **Your inner child likes everything to stay the same.**

- The status quo creates a sense of unity; *'united we stand, divided we fall.'* **Your inner child loves to feel safe.**

Would you like to add to the above list?

....

....

....

You may be wondering if the status quo ever changes their point of view:

The consensus appears to be yes… they do eventually – but only when there is enough momentum from within the group or when they fear a backlash from the membership if they don't change a particular stance/viewpoint.

Clearly there are benefits to living within the status quo and their conformity structures. This was sound reasoning when we were children, adolescents, teens and even young adults, but now the maturing individual is frustrated in his maturing needs, feeling 'stuck' and conforming with his fear of fear of rejection… nothing but mediocrity ahead.

22. LIVING WITHIN 'THEIR' BOUNDARIES

Let's take a closer look at how people 'appear' to have power over you:

Who makes you feel disempowered? How do they benefit?

....
....
....

How do you feel disempowered? What type of situations cause you to feel disempowered?

....
....
....

What's the energy like between you and your oppressor?

....
....
....

What do you do with your frustration? Do you vent your feelings or do you withdraw/avoid? Do you become angry with yourself?

....
....
....

Basically, controlling personalities use fear and rely upon your naivety and gentleness to work *for them – against you*. Fear and naivety become the bullies of the unconscious adult:

What phrases does your oppressor use to control you?

....
....
....

Who else, besides the status quo, intimidates you? What intimidates you?

....

....

....

Now let's add our free will to the mix.

23. THE STATUS QUO VS. YOUR FREE WILL

Most of us belong to the status quo! Again, belonging to 'the group' is part of our survival intelligence and our conditioning – the group helping us survive, always more powerful than the individual. It's a conditioned acceptance that this is how it works.

Now let's find out why conforming is difficult for some of us.

Highlight any of the following statements that ring true for you:

- 'Now with our evolving intellect, the 'one rule fits all' conformity expectation is illogical, especially as every individual is unique, compounded by our different backgrounds and experiences.'

- 'The status quo is stuck in time.'

- 'I feel my maturing needs cannot be met with their conformity expectations. There is no flexibility or negotiation.'

- 'They don't like new ideas or innovative thoughts – mediocrity rules.'

- 'There's no room for expansion. I feel 'stuck'.'

- 'I can't reach my potential with all their rules running my life.'

We now know how and where the 'one rule fits all' philosophy has its origins.

Is it time to liberate your spirit?

To do this, you must step up and go after what you want. The people who choose to live without the umbrella protection of the status quo are often those who make the revolutionary changes for society. Without their courage, there would be no great artists, writers, architects, scientists etc., who have advanced society. We should salute their courage!

I also believe some of the spectators living within status quo conformity secretly admire those brave souls. And remember: the status quo eventually accepts the great liberated spirits from the past who have advanced society.

Understand, the status quo will rarely change. You will be fighting 'the crowd' for the rest of your life. If you want something more or something different, then it's up to you to make it happen and live your life your way.

Realise: it's never about you. The people who oppose you and/or your progress or who resist your idea or a change in your behaviour, are living within 'their' beliefs and conformity expectations. They are scared, security conscious people who are protecting themselves and their position. They treat everyone who shows signs of dissident behaviour as a potential threat to their innate need for security and certainty. When you choose independence, you are disturbing their sense of security.

One more thing: it's never personal. Don't think for one moment, you are being singled out. The same treatment is dished out to everyone who threatens the status quo 'crowd psychology' in some way.

When you realise, all the rules and conditioning learnt in the first half of your life are no longer working for you, you need to let go

– even if you don't want to move away from the security of 'The Pack'. This is now your adult choice.

There is a conscious art to knowing how far you can push the boundaries with an individual or an institution that is on a different frequency and life path to you, without hurting yourself and compromising your health.

The good news: when you get to this level in your understanding, you will realise you don't need to ask for permission. It really is that simple. You are free to take the initiative and decide the best way to live your life, *with or without their approval.* It's the only reasonable and smart conclusion for anyone wanting to live beyond traditional conformity and mediocrity. *Bubbles anyone?*

Now let's understand how your courageous emotional bases will help you achieve your freedom.

Notes/challenges:

....
....
....
....
....
....
....
....
....
....
....
....
....
....
....
....
....
....
....
....
....
....
....
....
....
....
....
....
....
....
....

SECTION VI:

YOUR COURAGEOUS EMOTIONAL BASES

OVERVIEW: BEYOND YOUR FEAR OF 'FEAR OF REJECTION'

Let's sort out one of our most basic concerns i.e., what others may be thinking about us. We know this thinking began in childhood and was especially relevant in our teen years and has continued in one way or another since then.

Great news: you may be surprised to learn how infrequently people think about other people. Most of the time, they are totally consumed with themselves and their own problems.

Remember: most people are living through the literal beliefs of their childhood model which are survival-based, and therefore must be self-protective, 'personal' and serious. In other words: if there's been no self-enquiry or introspection, you are dealing with a literal child's conditioning, his fears, the need to belong and its conformity expectations, dependence, supposed tos, shoulds etc.

The following 'real-life' story is a perfect example of the fear of 'fear of rejection':

The fear of 'fear of rejection' created severe reactions for almost all my clients when I ran a classic glamour services business. The three-hour session was designed and created for each client and included anatomic make-up techniques, hairstyling to suit face shape and colours complimentary to skin tones from seasonal colour swatches.

After I had shown each client how they could transform their appearance, step by step over the three hours, they couldn't believe how beautiful they looked! After staring at the mirror for a minute or so, 90% would say, "I can't look like this!" They would mention their husbands like them to look 'natural', or their friends or family wouldn't like them looking like this.

Understand: fear of offending the VIPs in our life is a potent killer of free will.

My clients were choosing to live beneath their enhanced beauty for fear of upsetting someone important in their lives, perhaps fearing rejection or not feeling they were worthy or deserving of looking so beautiful.

So, the fear of fear of rejection, offending a VIP in our family or our generational need for acceptance is often more intimidating and difficult to overcome than our need to make our own choices and forge our own path.

Now, with your knowledge of the two time zones, and how most people are likely to react to any change in your behaviours, appearance etc., you may like to speak to their insecurity and explain to important others that the changes you are making are about you advancing to the next stage in your development. The changes are not against them… you still love them!

The #1 Fear: Fear of rejection

Fearing repercussions if we step away from our conditioning and decide for ourselves, is a perfectly understandable position in the first half of our lives.

Today you are working from an adult's intellectual perspective… you don't need anyone's approval to feel okay about yourself. If you want a bigger life, the possibility of rejection is part of the deal.

Please believe that it's okay not to be liked. Being liked by everyone is impossible and being liked per se is not a prerequisite for happiness given the mercurial tendencies of popularity. Liking yourself is your new benchmark.

Has fitting in and going along with group thinking, ever made you feel truly empowered? Be honest. Reasons:

....

....

....

What's the one thing you can do to help overcome your fear of fear of rejection?

....

....

....

I'm not suggesting for a moment that it's easy. Heaven knows, becoming emotionally independent is heroic! That's why so few people do it!

The 'live' subconscious cords we are about to disarm in the next chapter are your childhood and teenage need for acceptance.

24. DISARMING 'LIVE' SUBCONSCIOUS REACTIONS TO YOUR 'OLD' SELF- IMAGE

Again, let's start by separating the time zones:

The literal child and your teen identity:

Your beliefs about yourself, your self-esteem, sense of importance and self-worth were all formed in the first half of your life. Feedback was confirmed on an instinctual and emotional level by how others reacted to you. The literal child accepts all comments at face-value and your teenage time zone forms opinions about itself by how well it is accepted by its generation.

The unaware/reactive adult:

This adult continues to allow the opinions of others from an earlier time zone to validate his feelings of worthiness and identity today, all impacting his self-belief and confidence.

Empowered concepts:

The awakening adult is working with his new and empowered self-image, acknowledging his many skills, qualifications, life education, qualities, experiences, competence and wisdom today. He is no longer stunted by outdated, 'were they ever real' beliefs from an earlier time zone. He admits he is okay! and is a work in progress and loving it!

You are no longer the diminutive child or the conforming teenager! So, no more feelings of 'not enough' and self-doubts sabotaging your dreams before you've even started!

Let's build you an up-to-date, empowering self-image.

25. CREATING YOUR UP-TO-DATE ID – EMOTIONAL INDEPENDENCE

Your emotional independence from 'the group' is a major power base in your maturing life. You are admitting to yourself that with all your life experiences, life education, qualifications, wisdom etc. it's okay to be 'different'!

Unlike your childhood and teen years, where 'different' was a stigma and at odds with conformity, in your maturing years 'The individual' is an awesome power base. It is a breakaway from the traditional conforming mindset of your generation and the status quo… that we must all be the same!

***

First become aware of your internal dialogue i.e., the words and phrases you use regularly when speaking to yourself.

Note your words: Are they uplifting and encouraging, or do they diminish your adult image? Are any from an earlier time zone?

....
....
....

Note your phrases: Do they boost your confidence and encourage you, or do they have the opposite effect? Any from an earlier time zone?

....
....
....

Trying to direct your life today from an image that was created in your childhood and teen years and others' opinions of you, will not change your beliefs about you or build your confidence. Now it's about the importance of your inner world and the changes that appear in your exterior world when you are working with an up-to-date self-image, building confidence and new beliefs in yourself; making choices that work in your best interests today.

To help you *feel* the difference between the time zones, and to help align your self-image with current time, here's a wide range of uplifting words. Highlight the words that resonate with you or words you can grow into:

tenacious	considerate	passionate
conscientious	resourceful	lovable
optimistic	creative	assertive
courageous	honest	analytical
independent	thoughtful	loyal
decisive	gracious	inspiring
innovative	a leader	empathic

Any other image-building words?

....
....
....

From Chapter 19: Self-talk and affirmations, which affirmations did you highlight to encourage you to transcend your bodyguard and move forward?

....
....
....
....
....

Now it's time to think about who you are today. This is a grand opportunity to own up and embrace everything you have been silencing or not daring to consider. This is about creating an 'upbeat rave review' about you and your updated life qualifications. Include issues you have overcome, how proud you felt about yourself. Note your achievements. Who you want to be. What would this feel like/look like for you? Create a powerful self-image that will challenge you and change your destiny. Be courageous!

....
....
....
....
....
....
....
....
....
....
....
....
....
....
....
....
....
....
....

Where would you like to be in say a year's time, two years' time. Five years from now? Would you like to put a 'Statement of intent' together to help you stay on track?

....
....
....
....
....
....

Now let's build you a courage shopping list.

26. BUILDING YOUR COURAGE SHOPPING LIST – EMOTIONAL EXPANSION

Time to take your dreams from improbable to possible and then to actual.

The following quotation is again an excerpt from Marianne Williamson's beautiful quotation from her 1992 self-help book 'A Return to Love' and is so apt here:

"Your playing small does not serve the world. There is nothing enlightened about shrinking so that other people will not feel insecure around you. We are all meant to shine, as children do..."

Your courage shopping list:

Leave your question in plain sight for the next week or so and allow your thoughts and ideas to come through freely. Nothing is ruled out... forget fear and your old comfort zones, override all the things you were told you can't do or can't have. Include everything that you would love to have in your life, even things you consider imaginary or unobtainable. Think bold!

....
....
....
....
....
....
....
....
....
....
....
....

Project manage your life. See your life as something you are building:

- concentrate on one item at a time.

- visualise the result first, then backtrack from the result to where you are now. In other words: plan a series of tiny steps.

- keep your target in mind especially first and last thing each day and watch what happens.

Your thoughts injected with passion are like magnets. Like attracts like.

Now let's work with your subconscious to help your courage shopping list come into life.

27. HOW TO WORK WITH YOUR SUBCONSCIOUS MIND TODAY

This chapter is borrowed from Conscious: 'How life works':

What does the subconscious love to work with?

- repetition

- images

- passion and emotional intensity.

How are you contributing to your current situation?

When your subconscious hears you say repeatedly with passion and emotional intensity, things like:

- 'I'm always experiencing delays!' or

- 'I can never have what I want!' or

- 'I'm always in debt!'

Guess what? You will get more of the same. Your subconscious believes that is what you want! It's literal! It takes you at your word!

How to work with and benefit from your subconscious:

- become aware of your internal monologue

- use positive, *simple words that cannot be misinterpreted* – remember, your subconscious can be likened to a six-year-old child

- use short direct sentences/statements

- speak and feel with emotional intensity

- *speak in present time... as if you already have what you want*

- visualise images of yourself with the item you are seeking

- concentrate on one item at a time

- repeat your statement over and over every day – especially first thing in the morning and before you go to sleep

- continue repeating your statement, until you get what you want.

Be sincere. You can't trick kids on an emotional level, that's their language, and the language of your subconscious mind.

Don't decide how you think it should happen – your subconscious doesn't work with the intellect, rules, beliefs or traditional thinking. Watch out for the unexpected.

Don't decide how long it should take – your subconscious has no clocks or watches in its world.

Decide one thing you are seeking or wanting to change. Construct your short, passionate simple statement using the above format:

....
....
....

Your request is now out of your hands and your learnt controlling behaviour. Stay alert for clues. Be patient and keep the faith. Know your subconscious is dedicated to you and is doing everything in its power to deliver your wish. Let your subconscious do its job. Persistence and dedication wins!

A word of warning: Be careful what you wish for – your subconscious is serious and literal. Like a child, it takes you literally at your word.

28. THE RIGHT TO BE YOURSELF – EMOTIONAL EXPRESSION

We become disconnected and discontent with ourselves when our emotional life is not included in our busy schedule. *I know my 'intellectual only' life eventually became increasingly difficult and frustrating to live with. My life felt empty and stressed rather than filled with passion, joy and purpose.*

This is another reason why so many people change careers and lifestyles in midlife. They are done with the 'intellectual only' life and are going after a passionate, more emotionally satisfying life.

One way to do this, *without disrupting your life and involving your bodyguard,* is to diarise time for yourself. This has the added benefit of keeping you out of the resentment zone. Finding happiness in something you love to do adds precious emotional nourishment and satisfaction to your life, connecting you with your essence, fuelling your highs and lifting your lows.

As young children, we invented ways to play. In fact, playing and creating are ways we connect with our authentic selves.

Happiness enters your life in present time when you are working towards a goal or something you desire. It's the journey, not the destination that determines your state of happiness. Your bodyguard, of course, will always be part of your journey. ☺

If you've never experienced being 'in the flow' where time simply disappears or you've never felt sublime happiness and pure joy when you've been totally involved in something you love to do, then it's your duty to yourself to begin the search.

Dissatisfaction and boredom creep in when we are not creating, refreshing and rejuvenating our lives with love, vision and creative energy. Our imagination sustains us, building newness, making us feel happy and alive.

Do you have an emotional outlet? What makes you feel emotionally satisfied and nourished?

....
....
....

Is there any way you can turn this emotionally satisfying thing you do into a career move? How could you make it happen?

....
....
....

Your talent is another major power base. It is usually some kind of service rendered to others, giving you pleasure as you provide that service. In Greek mythology, it's called a blessing. Your blessing is your calling, your purpose, your life's work – the source of great happiness. Please don't waste your talents – we were all born with something special. Was there something you loved to do as a child or a teenager?

What happened to your talent? Were you told it was fanciful... that you should have an education. Was there an expectation you would follow in the family footsteps? Over the years, have you suppressed your talent? What role did your bodyguard play then/ now? What can you do to revive your talent?

....
....
....
....

....
....
....
....
....
....
....
....
....
....
....

There may be no need for a tertiary qualification for your talent, passion or calling but rather, gaining your constantly evolving qualifications through experience and practical 'life education'. Take some time and think about this.

Maybe you know a young person who has a natural skill. Can you support, encourage and nurture his talent?

***

To complete Marianne Williamson's beautiful quotation from her 1992 self-help book: *A Return to Love*, I have added the last few lines, again, so apt here:

"... As we let our own light shine, we unconsciously give other people permission to do the same. As we are liberated from our own fear, our presence automatically liberates others."

***

Thank you:

We've come a long way, haven't we? Power to you and the little kid in you in the 21st Century. May you transcend your childhood primal fear and its comfort zones and embrace the liberated, intellectual interpretation of fear as your personal bodyguard… standing alongside you, protecting you in all your endeavours.

Best wishes and the courage to pursue your potential through your emotional independence, emotional expansion and emotional expression. Thank you for your trust and support. I truly appreciate both.

***

Let's finish this journal with a salute to your backseat driver:

A TRIBUTE TO THE INNER CHILD

"I love my inner child's primal simplicity –
Her beliefs in the first seven years created our history.
My inner child believes she is all she can be...
She is the younger version of me.

I see everything through my inner child's eyes...
Her beliefs become my beliefs until I am wise.
She is dependent and powerless in every way –
I show her there's more when I 'shoo' fear away.

With her by my side I make perfect sense...
She is the substance, the heart and the core of my essence.
Our 'dream-team' consciousness transforms my identity.
I am complete and transcending my inner child's destiny."

Louise L. Kallaway.

Notes/challenges:

....
....
....
....
....
....
....
....
....
....
....
....
....
....
....
....
....
....
....
....
....
....
....
....
....
....
....
....
....
....

ADDENDUM:

REINTERPRETING THE MIDLIFE CRISIS

This Addendum adds a 'little bit extra' and is a perfect way to conclude *Survival*. I hope you like it.

My explanation, mostly borrowed from *Conscious,* will involve some repetition, but this deeper explanation will make even more sense of your life.

Around midlife we begin to feel 'stuck' leading to feelings of frustration. Let's investigate what the feeling of 'stuckness' really is from a 'whole of life' perspective.

What is 'stuckness'?

We feel stuck in old patterns, learnt coping behaviours, beliefs, attitudes, the fear of upsetting important others and our conditioned fear-based comfort zones, to name a few.

Where are we stuck?

- We are stuck in our learnt behaviours and conditioning.

- Stuck in childhood fear-based comfort zones.

- Stuck in old coping behaviours such as avoidance and blaming.

- Stuck in the 'black-or-white', 'yes-or-no', either/or world of a child.

- Stuck in our teenage generation's conformity issues.

- Stuck in our need for acceptance above self-acceptance.

Any others?

....

....

....

Why are we feeling stuck?

When our intellectual brain took over around seven-years-old, it was given priority above our feeling/emotional life and has remained in the #1 position as we continued fitting-in and conforming in the first half of our lives:

- By the age of 21, we are physically fully developed.

- Our intellectual brain continues to restructure and rewire itself until around 25 years of age.

- Now, in midlife, our emotional life (right-side brain) wants to catch up to *her* fully developed physical and intellectual counterparts, giving us choices that expand our world and move us forward into the adult rite of passage... if we have the courage.

> *Your emotional life is the backbone of your life.*
> *She, your right-side emotional brain, is your courage.*
> *He, your left-side intellectual brain, is your reasoning.*

Now, in midlife:

We've been conditioned to think that if we make an independent decision that goes against the status quo and our teenage generation and 'their' group conformity expectations, then we must be having a midlife crisis! *Not true... never been true!*

What is really happening is:

- **We've outlived the primitive, reactive/kneejerk survival system.**

- **We've outgrown our conditioning and all its rules, conforming and fitting-in as we did in the first half of our lives.**

- **Midlife has no (new) rules! Only the old rules and our conditioning we drag into current time from the past.**

Today, 'The individual' is free to claim his heroic and rightful place in history, choosing self-acceptance above the need for group acceptance, generational and status quo conformity expectations and its forces of mediocrity.

MORE REASONS TO INCLUDE YOUR FEELINGS:

When you dismiss the value of your emotional life, you become disconnected from your inner life. Your intellect bases its information on outside sources. If you haven't included your feelings in the decision making, h*ow do you know if the decision is right for you?*

I know my 'intellectual only' decisions eventually became increasingly difficult and frustrating to live with. My life felt empty and stressed rather than filled with passion and purpose.

This is another reason why so many people change careers and lifestyles in midlife. They are done with the 'intellectual only' life and are going after a more passionate and emotionally satisfying life. They are incorporating and trusting their feelings and their solar plexus chakra 'soul' connection, resonating and confirming their new direction.

Remember, your intellect is the new kid on the block – it had no part in your survival and still doesn't – the subconscious does the work in the first seven years, as it always has and as it always will!

When we don't include all three powerbases i.e., physical, emotional and intellectual, we feel out of balance and disconnected with ourselves.

I believe this is why we seek comfort in drugs, comfort in alcohol, comfort in food and/or comfort in excessive amounts of sex (you may disagree with the latter).

I know when I'm out-of-balance, I feel:

- Disconnected from my physical self.

- Disconnected from my emotional life.

- With only my over-functioning, overloaded intellect running the show, I go to the pantry and/or the fridge. I'm not admitting to any others ☺

To harmonise with those three systems, try giving each a say in your day-to-day transactions with yourself.

It doesn't get better than this! From the moment we were born, we are blessed with everything working for us, always in our best interests, always looking after us helping us survive when we understand 'The system' and 'How life works'.

REINFORCING… NO SUCH THING AS A MIDLIFE CRISIS:

Superficially, when we see anyone with greying hair buying a sports car or a muscle car, for example, it does look like delinquent adult behaviour, doesn't it? But what is really happening is those courageous maturing adults are transcending their fear of fear of rejection, making heroic choices that embrace their emotional independence from group conformity expectations. *We should salute their gutsy, proactive behaviours.*

Your V8 power is also found under the bonnet i.e., in your inner life. It is the adult's rite of passage to make choices that work in your best interests today – with or without your generation's okay and/or status quo approval.

Affirmation:

"I give myself permission to ....
....
.... **"**

ABOUT THE AUTHOR

Hello there! My interest and fascination into 'The system' we were born into began in my difficult teenage years.

My Mum and her little brother, aged 4 and 3 respectively, were made Wards of the State in New South Wales, Australia, during the Great Depression. Abruptly taken from their family home, remembering abandonment is a primal fear to a child, you can imagine the two little kids' terror and confusion as they were passed to an unfamiliar carer. I would love to give them a big hug and assure them, wouldn't you?

"Why did you bring us up the same way you were brought up when it hurt you so much?", I remember asking my Mum when I was 16. *"How else was I supposed to bring up you kids? It's the only way I know!"* was her emotional retort!

My curiosity was piqued. My 16-year-old's question: *'how can I prevent history repeating itself?'* became my adult question: *'Why do generational cycles repeat themselves?'* Thirty years later, the last pieces in life's giant jigsaw completed the puzzle!

***

When I began my research, I had no idea that my discoveries would disrupt anything! I simply wanted to understand why my mother repeated her harsh and insensitive childhood to her innocent children, so I wouldn't automatically repeat my upbringing to my innocent kids.

***

Over time it has become increasingly apparent that acceptance of my research and its discoveries would mean a complete overhaul, update and re-education to many tertiary qualifications, including mental health and early childhood development, among others. To ignore evolving discoveries and to pretend this research does not exist, is what the status quo does. No offense intended – that's its job! – continuing to keep us safe, living within 'The Pack' and its conforming 'pack' mentality, maintaining 'order' and resisting change of any kind, and so… perpetuating mediocrity.

We remain part of the status quo when we choose to remain silent, above making a difference in our community or by making better or more empowering choices for ourselves.

Without people like you, who are willing to investigate new research and new possibilities, the world will remain stagnant in the hands of the status quo. If this Journal has helped make sense of your primal fear, imagine how it could help others understand their fear and their feelings of 'stuckness' and powerlessness, and help liberate people who have 'settled' for a mediocre life.

I may be contacted at: www.linkedin.com/in/louise-l-kallaway or through my website: www.louiselkallaway.com

***

Having difficulty locating any of my 'Life education' books or journals? Please go to my website where you can order direct. Thank you again, Louise.

www.ingramcontent.com/pod-product-compliance
Lightning Source LLC
Chambersburg PA
CBHW050819090426
42737CB00021B/3438